Rain in a Dry Year

Rain in a Dry Year

Poems

by
Michael J. S. Forsyth

To my mother, who taught me what words were, and to my sister, who taught me what they meant.

———————————————————————————————

"Be like the fox, who makes more tracks than necessary, some in the wrong direction: practice Resurrection."
-Wendell Berry, *Mad Farmer Liberation Front*

"...but set down this set down this: were we led all that way for Birth or Death?"
-T.S. Eliot, *The Journey of the Magi*

"To the mountains rising above you: you should say...move. You will say move."
-Derrick C. Brown, *Blazing the Valley in Psalms*

TABLE OF CONTENTS

LAMENTATIONS 1
   Waiting for the Rain 3
   Flesh 6
   Battered Roses 7
   Teiresias 8
   Love 10
   Childhood 11
   Life is Very Long 12
   Wasting Out 13
   Pray for Rain 14
THE DRUNKEN DAYS 17
   Ode to the 40oz. 19
   Beloved Beauty 20
   The Obscene 21
   Becoming Drunk 22
   New Eyes 24
   Office Space 26
   Far from Rising Saints 27
   Epsiloning 28
   Gold-spun Soul 30
   Home 31
   Top-Blown-Off Boys 32
   Exhaustion 34
THE END OF THE WORLD 35
   Et Incarnatus Est 37
   The End of the World 38
   The Mediatrix 39
   Beauty Feared 40
   Meteor 41
   Sing Soft for Jane 42
   Words 43
   Home #2 44
   Beginning 45
   The Length of Time 46
   Mississippi Rain 47
   George Armand 48
RAIN IN A DRY YEAR 49
   Christmas 2013 51
   Morning glories 52
   Orange Oleander 53

A Theory of Parallels 54
Geometrical Researches 55
Reflections rather than reading Darwin 56
3:30 and Tomorrow 57
Finality 60
Ash Wednesday 61
Rain in a Dry Year 63
THE POET'S PRAYER 67
The Poet's Prayer 69
A Flame 70
How to Write 71
Lady of the Sea 75
California 76
Somedays 77
Morning 81
Santa Paula Creek 82

Lamentations

Waiting for the Rain

I. Santa Paula

Days like today spit delineation at you.

>Trees lose meaning in their leaves,
>>and shadows become demarcations of their
>makers.

>The thing I love about this land
is the way the mountains gallop stallion-like
>>into the plumed pacific, crashing

>Fire-white on the remains of men
>And fish
>>And vegetation –

But today is cut-glass

>shard-straight. Today is
>measured out and stuck

Like marble in its place,

And separation
>wraps itself round everything.

II. Highway 150

>>I fold everything I see into
>a story, and so

>I cannot bear to see the world unbent, but

now

Everything is laid brightly
        bare before my eyes:

        Every atom begs to have a proper name –

I cannot give them this.

III. Ferndale Ranch

I watch the sun
        battle with the storm, on-coming,

        Slowly bleeding from the
Top of Topa-Topa, crawling out like
        claws over the mountains,

And watch the gloom
lick away the day.

Winds blow
                all my friends
        inside
like dead leaves raked into a pile, but

here I will remain;

        stubborn in my
           home beneath the sycamores,

Eyeing angrily the last collapse
           of day; becoming brutal,

                I will raise myself into

an obscene gesture
aimed at mother nature:

     I am waiting
     for the rain.

Flesh

It is the feel of warning in the air,
The sound of hands crossed, crossing
Prayer with poetry; the turn from sound to honesty,
And loss of self in loss. I worry out these words
From parapets of paper, like fretted silk:
I dream out tapestries of self,
Have written wings onto my back
And soared up over
Smoke-stack chimney-lands
To settle in the rafters of reality.

But Flesh will not inherit.

Flesh of Flesh, my Flesh,
My blood, bloody, my bloodied Flesh
Blood swallowed by my flesh...
Abel's heart was eaten by the earth,
As will soon mine:
Earth becoming flesh becoming Dust, and,
At the hour of thy death
Be blown to dust.

"A sailor on the sea took my heart away from me"
"A lover on the land let me run off with her hand."

(Flesh will not
inherit)

But Jesse found the birch tree
Bowed.

Battered Roses

The corner of the page is folded down,
A frown reflecting burdened haste; A gown;
A dark, celestial tear upon the face
Of Beauty's form in Love's unkind embrace –
And I am grown to love all I must hate.
If only I could force myself to stay,
Retreat, and see time truly as a day…
I think I would not long for Time to wait.
But have I long to wait for time? I think
That better would it be to work in haste,
To stretch my hand to you, and hide my face –
If faced with awestruck eyes – for life's a blink,
And battered roses broken on the floor
Are better than warm beds and hollow cores.

Teiresias

I have crawled in depths of blackest night,
Climbed peaks impassible
In highest ecstasy;
I have passed beneath great archways
In caverns far below the world,
And lost track of time while traveling
Through endless space.

On worlds where wills abounded,
Where thoughts were real, and eyes blinked deep
Into the moonlit night,
I searched for something hidden
In the cloak of my desire.
Now I seek with ears the truths of passers-by,
What makes them personify
Being. I seek God in the squeal of new shoes,
The beat of footfall breaths.

Oh, endless night. My eyes are dead to me...
I wish to see your face once more,
See your sunken eyes, your wrinkled face,
Close you in my arms, and die.

Mine eyes...
My friend,

Have you seen my eyes?

But still, I stutter – day-dream walk
Through static sorrow,
Human-heavy breathing
Pacing back and forth before these windows I call ears.
I can find no beauty in their kind;
No, I see nothing here, within my twilight world
But misery and hate.

I lie here, how long, in blackest night?
Millennia compounded on millennia?

Soon, Perhaps I shall no longer be encased –
I do not mind to die...

...and yet, shall I still-crawling
call across that river
In like tongue?

I fear to find the dust will settle softly.

Remember,
Man,
That thou...

...Create, and end.

Love

You have witches in your eyes, dear girl;
Witches in your eyes, and silver in your hair –
Moonlight freckles in your hair;
Now rub the witches from your eyes, dear girl;
Leave the silver in your hair.

Dawn creeps quiet to your eyes, dear girl;
The sun sneaks 'cross your golden hair –
Flowing, flaxen, silky hair;
Rub your ready morning eyes, dear girl,
Run your new hands through your hair.

You are Mars beneath my eyes, dear girl,
Mars beneath my eyes, and red dawn in my hair –
Sailors drowning in my hair;
Calm the storm beneath my eyes, dear girl,
Wash the sea-foam from my hair.

Childhood

If I were to write my childhood days,
To hold my life within a pen,
What would I write?
…what could I write?
Would I chart the sands of Africa,
The taste of death, and of malaria?
Would I paint the heat of Trinidad,
Or the snow of '94?
Or should I speak of sitting in the hall,
Alone in worlds of picture-books?
I do not know...
And what of baseball? And scraped knees?
Or of my father shoveling the snow,
And dragging us to Rectory Hill
Where all the children laughed their quick ways down?

No. I think my soul, when all alone,
Dwells most upon that day
So warm, when warm winds stopped caressing me.
I wish to write of black suits far as eye could see
When, through my tears, I could see it all…
And of the rosary beads my father held
And of the man who wore suspenders
Ringing out the Star of Texas.
I will write of when, embarrassed, Jane and I
Pushed flowers across the floor.

Life is Very Long

Where are the stars tonight?
Where is Saturn, or the fire of Mars?
I feel cold, and left in the cold dark.
Shrouds ring out like bells
Around the cool, familiar springs.

What a night, to dance the old, familiar dance
We once employed,
A night to dream of pasts, and sing of love;
Life's a parchment upon which
Every day some new idea is written,
And then scratched out by desolating dusk.

Time is such a short amount of time to wander down some
unforsaken path,
Where every moment stops, and asks,
"Which way is home?
Where goes this road?"
I think that all loves are loves of the past,
As down I march through arch and stair,
To unnamed rooms where frightened stares
swirl like unbeggetting smoke
puffed from lipstick mouths.
What do I live,
Some sweet romance, or a sonnet, or
Something less...
I see often my father's grass.

We walk with nailed feet;
We stumble, and we fall.

Wasting Out

I do not desire death.
"Of course," you say. "No man does."
But death... I don't mean death.
Substantial Change, they call it, jumping
Between being, and... non,
Rabbit-like, bounding off across the fields of
Another distant world... or
Nothing.
This is not what I despise.

Rather, the weakening heart,
Slowing blood, brain addled, softened –
And walking with a cane...
I abhor the loss of speech,
And damn the loss of sight:
My sense, my mind,
My words deeds hopes dreams –
They all make me. And oh, losing that all-terrible
Desire, That all-lusting will...
What then will I be? Used up,
An old rag, soaked with
Too much liquor,
Tattered, frayed – what more, then, to be done
But throw away?

Yes, this is what I fear – the long, drawn,
Wasting out.
The subtle slips, the slow decay
Till, finally, shitting my own pants,
Lying in a hospital bed from which I cannot rise.
I count each blip upon the monitor
Like sheep to help me die.

Oh, I do not fear the death – I fear the dying.

Pray for Rain

"Pray for rain."
We pray; dry
cracked – we parch,
We are parched,
We become thirst;
Thirst me –

Pray for rain.
If sudden sparks ignite –
But how my stomach swells... Dried, I
Stutter, stick, scrape,
And I am strung

Pray for rain –
Prayer is praise of self.
We endure – enkindle me,
I move more, am moved more,
Remain the same – less the longing,
More the want.
Dried, drawn, dragged through
Scrub-oak-red-wood-rage
I rage against the coming.
Build the blaze.

Pray for rain.
I have prayed and I have praised,
I have knelt, and beaten breast,
Have sighed, wept, summed up, counted
Every crack and crinkle in my soil
But still my hillsides brown,
My oceans mourn

Pray for rain Why
Pray?
We have eternal summer – joy.
Heatstroke.

Grass left ungreened three years.
The cattle slowly snort through
Snot-encusted nostrils...
So much for good years

Pray for rain but
Pray? I have prayed.
Each day I dust my knees,
Sift through soil,
Breathe prayer muttered breathe
Raging prayer
Breathe prayer to rage against.
My eyes are salt, and
Curse this land I love;

"Pray for rain."

We will pray.

The Drunken Days

Ode to the 40oz.

By The Snoozer-Boozer-Loser
(As published in the Weekly Dirt)

Oh Muse of ever-present sighs,
Of memory of good days gone by,
Recall to me that sweetest smell
Of High Life (®) in a bottled well;
I first did see my object, tall,
$2.50 'gainst a frigid wall;
And yearning for that higher taste
Did reach to take, and taking, slake
My thirst for some much-higher hop;
My hope for some much-better stock –
I slaked my thirst for Heaven's crops.

Remember, Muse, that first dear hiss,
When bottle's cap and bottle's twist
Divorced the closed and did expose
The golden glow of honey's flow!
Oh, what great dreams were made in thee?
And what great thoughts? And what great deeds?
Dear Forty tall, I have, in thee,
The Hopes of all Mortality!
And thus concludes my joyful song:
For curfew calls – and I must run!

Beloved Beauty

In the whisper of the oak leaves,
In winter's coldest light,
The bare-boned breath of branches
Clung like claws to frozen flight;
And the mask of sharpest day
Tore the eyes of darkest night.

Oh my sweet, beloved beauty,
I have lived to praise your name –
In the coldest sheets of snow-fall,
In the quiet cough of day;
In the cough of quiet longing
I saw life, I saw decay.

In the wailing of the city,
In coiling, rippling hordes,
I saw resurrected romance,
Hatred hard, and old age, bored;
I saw glory in the striking
Of the sun upon the thorns.

Oh my sweet, beloved beauty
I have lived for your name's sake;
In the quiet of the chapel,
In the thund'ring, drunken rage;
In the sorrow of the graveside,
In the joyful light of day.

The Obscene
A poem in solidarity with the Phoenicians many miles from here

Draw upon the wrinkled,
Draw out into that fulsome,
Spread and drown your freckled,
Feathered substance in the deep...
Water drips, and, filtered, fills the
Disappointed with a shaking rage –
"Shake out that severed shadow from thyself:

The butcher ravels lies like meatstrings."

A rattled break of man – hands
Tied too fast to horror –
An aphrodisiac. The palpable sense
Of some nonsight suckles souls
The wrong way out. Keen to light
The sconce of self, a sheen so
Sudden, slick as lightning, creeps through the door –
In, the wicker man.

He licks the candle dry, licks light,

Snakelike. The drowned, undrowns,

And burns eternal night.

Becoming Drunk

So, let's be
Drunk.
Let's become obscenities,
Blasted on the corners
Of flipped-over, unremembered
Pages.
Spell it out:
If someone read these words...

But Nietschze says
"Care not" I –
Care not?
I care, in caring, loose
My everything, spread
It out like old houses,
Creaking, creasing, summer homes
Swept back by what
Could have been.

Speech quickly drowns.
Sleep gentle at her side,
Draw gently upon her
Grammatical, her
Psychological...
Elipses are more easily
Set down than commas:
We both are broken hinges.

To set forth:
First, the comma dies,
Replaced by rage,
Recounted in announced persuasion.

Next: Even words, impossible to write.
Perhaps my end's blossom will betray
Some inner sight, some

Being deep within
My Kosmos.
Now that, that was something,
Something that I thought was real.
Long time ago.

Somehow,
I counter-weave,
Relapse; and raise myself –

In splendor.

New Eyes

1.
Too many lights,
Too many sounds are swirling round and round and round
And now I cannot see, I cannot hear,
My breath it trumpets like the king.
Light is not for long,
Our time fades.

2.
The moon is belly-up,
Is full tonight, as all around is firelight
And shattered stars...
Somehow my heart is tied,
Look:
With singing eyes.

3.
I laugh with each new beating,
Each lying life-line in her swirling, twirling dress
And now I feel oh so much more
Alive
To live always Alive
To live always at dusk...
This is how it seems, at least for this last night,
For all this clamping air brings peace
With every thought, as it returns.

4.
Nay, my bones are not yet
Cold though all around is
Cold – I am warm?
Bah – You speak too much.

5.
I will revive this youth,
This newborn infant, undefiled but still beautiful
Unlike the tarred, that
Is IT. I am not no nothing no more.
No not now, now is not time.

Nothing knows newness but new eyes.

6.
Clocks are Slinking
Night is Feeling
Light is Clinking
Time is Treading
I am Killing
Night is Dark and Cold and
Love.

7.
Breathe for me, new eyes. Breathe.

Office Space

This poem is an ode
To the crystal click-clack of
Chipped nails on keyboards.
This poem is an ode
To the rat-tat beat of broken dreams
Drowning in luminescent fluorescent forever-gray-cubicled
Undersea. No wonder
We're all fat here. The pressure
makes our bones mushy just like blobfish
And when the A/C gives out our brains drip down
Our sleeves. We live
8 hours daily sitting in a tin can dry air
Perfume gloating
Necktie choking
Kraka-whirr printer humming
80s hair-metal blasting three rows down
World – LIVE YOUR LIVES AGAIN!

I wonder if you can.
I wonder if your puffy eyes ever
Held a dream,
If computer-screens have made you color-blind
Or if you wailed out this pastel world at birth.
I wonder if the jutting ridges of your life
Had to be shaved off to fit inside
Your cubicle.
I wonder if you've ever heard a freight train humming past
And thought of home...
I wonder if this
Is what I should call home.

Far from Rising Saints

Violet blurs, calls cater-wauled – scenery
Shaded, folded over, spilled out
Slowly though the years: lost in swerving nights,
I am thrown towards endless pasts –
Smeared, scraped, cluttered homes
Of dreams – heads masked,
Tired; sullen; gin sipped straight, till,
Laughing, bells peal, rung out –
Strung out masks trample
In unbodied gloom;
We sung about the moon, the reckless
Passing of two eyes, and,
With my eyes on you, I dreamt of hopeful pasts
As yet to come, but, coming, long will last.

But, for now, these streets fill me with fear –
Fear, fire-flung, drowned in salty worlds,
Struck like seasons, stuck on thunderous souls;
Fear, for far I stand from fields,
Blood rushing, hands thrust above for faith;
Far, I
Stand far from rising saints.

Epsiloning

For Isak Bond

You say you see the future in my eyes –
How nice. I hope it seems
Clear, straightforward,
Derived, decided, set down,
And absolutely uttered.
"Let it be written:" Let it.
Write a million words – can they be done?
There's the rub. Rubbed – that's me.
Thats us. We... fools.
Shouting out our hearts into the wind,
Reckoning our words against
Our Creator –

But Who
Spoke
First?

My speech begins and ends –
Alphas, with His breath,
Epsilons, deltas, gammas
(or whatever)
Omegas into Him.
Every word I speak's been said...
Said a thousandfold, a
Billionfold.
But can I stop? I –

Sicken me.

So, write, Yes,
Write, read, dream think
Burn. Oh, all will burn, at last –
All will burn,
And so, when you and I both stand

Before that final flaming pyre
Of all the stupid shit we ever said
And ever held so dear –
Will we remember this?
This hour minute
Second
That you said
"The Creator loves our words?"

The sun descends, and from
A mountain, afterglowing,
I hear a voice bombarding down
The wrinkles and the ridges of this land
That I have made my home:
It tells me son,
My Son,

You wait upon a word.

Gold-spun Soul

Twitching stomach, sorrow hair,
Rainy gravel and plip-plop drops of rain...
I feel the day dawn like open cans.
We welcome lovely days like Sunday parades,
And slip our lowly sliding souls down to the shore
But Oh, I love you more
Than words could ever speak, than
Silence could even say;
I miss in just one simple day
Your green-gray eyes,
Your golden hair, gold-spun soul;
I dream your dreamy skin,
Your ringing speech – one day and all that I can think
Is you...

The water pours in draughts, and then
Like bees.
I smell your scent like –
Lilies.

Oh, I long for night,
For cavalcades and empty speeches on some stage,
For less-than-sober dance and dreamy stares...
For you.
I count each second.

Home

I have spoken Dark,
Painted Death against a shadowy wall,
Chained myself, and shut the door;
I have dreamed Despair, and spoke his tongue –
I speak it still –
And I have walked the valley in fear.

But what is this new color
Mixed and muddled out of
All these pastel paints,
Dawning on the easel of my life?
I have looked for it before,
Tried to fake its brilliant, simple strains...

It is the shade of sober Friday nights at home,
In bed by midnight, reading
Dostoevsky, or Hopkins,
After laughing with my mother about
Our not-so-chilly years,
And hearing my sister play some sweet note on her guitar,
Singing Norah Jones...
It is the relief of pain from my father's death,
From my family's curse.

This is the first time since I was eight
I have felt myself at home.

Top-Blown-Off Boys

Those champagne top-blown-off boys
Flew like thunderclaps at spat-blood rooftops,
Beat like ruts, like cast-off
Cut-ups,
Beat down rain like rebel yell
Into their gutters.
Oh, those boys flew fast like moments,
Screeching round the gravel road in those
Souped up jacked up pickup trucks
They tried to turn their junkyard scrap into.

Oh, time ROARED past like records –
Beats.
Bass.
Beer.
And dancing's always better after
Drinking prayers.
I laughed a lot back then...
At painted nails traded for a smoke,
At trying to find a buck on Sunday nights before the shop closed,
At Jerusalem being closer than my home,
Dancing on the Dinos,
Driving drunk, and being broke,
Jumping naked in the hot springs,
And singing songs like lion-roars;

Oh, we roared in just like lions,
And went out whisper-lambs...
With shorn wool:
With holes in our hearts,
And in our heads,
And in our arms;
With sheet-metal shakes
And hidden scars...

Last night yesterday felt a whole lot better.

Oh, those champagne top-blown-off boys...
They shot the Moon –

And Smacked

      into the sky.

Exhaustion

I shake the storm,
The corner of the morn
Cuts through the corner of the glass,
Like eyes – downcast – flutter
Gently, for an instant in a laugh;
The flutter past, the fog refills the window-pane:
And I turn back to sleep.

The End of the World

Et Incarnatus Est

Here I bring you – stamping,
Tramping down the fallow fury of the age
The cracks and crags of peaks unpassioned,
Anger unemployed,
Will, unwilling love, loving lack of will;
Engendered gorily, for grandeur gross,
Glory grasping blood
From empty shells of shadows –
Here I bring half-beast, half…
not.

Et in…

I bring a beast, Half-bright,
A wailing whelp of wont, a constant gaze –
Sight un-seeing, dragging down
The breath-scraped bruise of twilit-sky –
Dragging down a deluge, to drown
The bleeding earth – to
Annihilate that earth.

Et incarnat…

I hear a bell ring quiet, through the quiet;
The day drifts through the thorns.

Et incarnatus est.

The End of the World

Dawn blew in, brisk and brittle
As the breach of love's first kiss;
Tugging on its mother's sleeve
In fear, did hide itself behind the clouds,
The clouds that layered up, and up, and up against the sky,
A bruise upon the firmamental brow;
It broke, a whimpered, sighing,
"Oh."

And in that final syllable, that whisper of a breath
That bore this all to life,
That breath that brought to light the stars and all the twirling
spheres,
That burned the earth with scorching light
Of suns and Sons,
That breath that soared above the deep

Blew the candle out.

The Mediatrix

The Grace of God, that spans against the sky,
That mantle, pure; that effervescent night
Of nights – that night, when Life was won, when sight
Did blind all sense, and blinding, sparked the cry;
The shimmer, stark, called light into my mind,
While up against that mantle, darkest blue –
Or not – sky warmest – warm as sunrise-dew,
The strength of caused did circle to unwind
The blasting down of Beauty, filling souls
With bursting girth of will, to light the coals;
And bursting coals, to praise the mother sky,
That brought to grace, with grace, both you and I;
Thou Mediatrix Mother, through thee shines
The Love of God, without which love, I die.

Beauty Feared

I yearn to hold your face between my hands,
To feel your beauty feared; to trust to touch,
For eyes, nor ears, nor smell could sense enough –
Destroyed in too-full faith; In battered brands
Of burn, and bright. In yearning for a light
I found, at last, a day: a night, a wind…
You shook me from my last, my mortal binge:
You shook my whole, and took my heart afright.
But what will I? What will? How will? How might?
I dreamt in love the mind was in the touch,
I dreamt the sigh was sign of 'hold,' 'enough;'
I will meet minds, and hearts, and skin the sight,
In seeing, hear; in hearing, feel the fright
Of Godhead seen divine, in eyeless flight.

Meteor

I saw a star in fickle flight
Come crashing down the other night;
It burst into the atmosphere,
A ball of gas, a searing sight;
It fell into my open arms,
It fell about a year ago;
And burnt my heart, and stole my soul,
And damned my open road:

I saw my fickle star in flight
From all that it once knew,
And it did burst the soul in me,
And rent past wounds anew.

Sing Soft

for Jane

Sing soft, dear sister, soft and smooth,
Sweet as your first day;
Dry your eyes, my sister dear,
Leave the troubled grave.

Sing sweet, dear sister, sweet and low,
Eyes as new as dawn
Dawn to dusk, and dusk to dawn,
What comes has quickly gone.

Sing smooth, dear sister, smooth and sweet,
As sweet as newborns' tears;
Yes, sing for me a lullaby,
And I will write one here.

Sing strong, dear sister, strong and true,
As true as your first smile –
I love you so, my dearest friend,
I love your heartwarm smile.

And now, sing soft, dear sister, friend,
For Love has conquered thee
Love that swiftly floods the soul
And sets the singer free.

Words

Carousing in my mind
Beating breaking battering biting
Orgying – one moment
One, and then another,
And another and another and another
And then – gone.
Gone like snow in summer,
Gone like youth,
Gone like
Those I thought I loved –
Gone
Like the weekend
When Monday morning comes.

Home #2
for Z.

You drew yourself a home on the bathroom wall,
Because you said the one where you grew up
Was always drifting away from you.
Maybe that's why, sometimes, you'd leave –
Take off in the middle of the night, unannounced – just
To make sure it was still there, hadn't fully faded back,
maybe... maybe you kept going back to see
If their hearts had broken yet. I get that.
When I am old and worn, and spend my hours
Counting off past days like worn-down rosary beads,
I hope to find one heart that burst apart.
Just one.
Maybe broken hearts is what home really is –
I know you found one, you might not realize, not yet,
Just what you did that night,
That night you drew on the bathroom wall
With the ink you found in your veins.

Beginning

Times, and, times before –
Before the sun and moon and stars
Danced the evening-song of love,
Before that stretch salvific,
Arms spread out open-wide;
Before that beginning began to be –
I began beginning.

What cosmic crush?
What remnant, what ferment found,
What force filled the void? I began
Before the all, that all-lusting
Begot itself towards me,
And in each drawing, drew its
Bootstrap-up self.

Match, striking, flame
Shakes out, draws brow,
Spark meets spark, together
Bursts at once into an omni-glow –
That is the first.
I start in sour, in
Subtle touch and sting,
Flame out, and dance cross
Shining gossamer-glory
Strings that join the far
To now...

All joined, all a burgeoned
Bright, all
A Massive and a One.

The Length of Time

The length of time, from then till now,
From smile to tear, from laugh to furrowed brow
That rips bare all the talk of other days,
Of youth, when you and I played laughing
In the mud on days of rain;
The length, from tossing sleep to shuddering rage
At all this time poor-spent, and all that drunken age;
The vast expanse between this seat and you, my friend,
And caught up in the trouble of the deep;
The length between my father's life and death,
My birth, and then, my peace
With all the world, with broken heart, and me,
Is but a shadow on this silly page;
Yet more than that – it is an "all" before that All
In which we slink like snakes until we find
A glimpse of dawn to wrestle,
To beat us down, and drown us in the deep;
And wrench us back, awoken from our sleep.

Mississippi Rain

She smelt like sugar-cane,
like wet, rising off
The concrete in a summer
Rain I met in Mississippi one
Murky day, or
Maybe summer itself.
She smelt like summer, underneath
Her fingernails, and, most of
All, behind her ears.

Her words turned me to coals.

George Armand

You sucked the concrete right out of my
Heart. Unbeat, beating in a reckless cameo –
I, a straw, flame up like embers.
So, he said, George Armand said, 15 years
Spent warmed by not much more than dirt.
Oh, San Francisco, your fog and wet lays
Deep within my heart – I remember looking out
The window at 160 – the white-washed,
Far too often repainted – Trust me, now I know
The smell of mold painted over all too well – and
Caught a whiff of life bulging in the fog.
It birthed me. That year spent doused in
Oblivion called my mortality to become mortal,
And shrugged a wreck onto its shore.

Rain in a Dry Year

Christmas 2013

It was a simple thing – as
All great things are.
Dawn stretched out, gasping
At the last retreat of gentle night,
A man emerged to feed the pigs
And flung the slop into their trenchers,
A child overturned the milk-bucket
In his haste to flee the nervous cow.
The king lay thickly in his bed,
And the watchmen on the walls
Thought of whores and money lost at dice-
A woman brought the laundry to the stream.

A man's gaze searched his newborn son for signs
That all that once was old, was made again.

Morning glories

She planted morning-glories in the yard.
She planted cabbage, carrots,
Rhubarb,
But the morning-glories she said she planted,
"Just in case."

I could have kissed her there, right there,
When she told me that – could maybe even
Could have even maybe loved her. Loved
Entirely, eyes to marrow.

I don't know if I've ever seen a morning-glory,
At least, if I have, I've never known –
I picture them as brass trumpets blowing in
The blood-red gusty dawn, glowing
Fiery with a glory untouchable.

They look
Like purple faces.
A bit of a let-down, to be honest,
But, I think
That's a bit nicer.
Smiling in each day.

My father planted morning-glories in the yard,
In our backyard in Virginia
When I was very young. They were his favorites.
I remember, in a dusky memory – one of those
Morning memories, I think – seeing him
Pruning the vine.

I think that was the year he lost his job and started
Losing life.

Orange Oleander

Orange oleander flees in flashes
Back, and sinking into
White-warm yellow branches, burns in streetlamp
Moth-collections – we sweep past
In warm-night winter, blown
Towards living, life, and lively longing, back
To broken breaths and
Bleeding days.

This day has been replaced
By soft-warm blanket golden,
Softer, warmer blue on the horizon – Topa-Topa
Towering on the edge
Of sight, scraping on a sky
Caught like clothing hung against that
Homeland mountain – each ravine a fold,
Inviting me to climb, to stare upon
The cloudy-chorused night,
To be entrapped within the chorus of the night,
And be a part of every sleepless sigh.

At once, we stop; the lights turn off, and
Silence speaks the symphony of time;
Shadows stand, the aloe vera glows –
Kind, cold – reminds me of the wind-break trees at sunset
Scouring the blood-swept sky,
As we flew by the fields of oranges and avocados.

A Theory of Parallels

Russia and Germany
England and Spain
I on the beach
And you in the waves
The stars in the night
And the planets aligned
Become protons and neutrons
Held together by light
And tomorrow is dust
But from dust man was born
In that early blue twilight
The cosmos was formed
And our hearts all were forged
In stars dying of fright
So when I look deep in you
I see tears in your eyes
I see ants on a leaf
And a house being built
I see birds on the wing
And the earth on its tilt
The child at dawn
And the old man at dusk
Hitler repeating
Napoleon's thrust
But Time won't repeat,
Though it rhythms and rhymes,
Turns us all into fools
Every day left behind
For the warmth of the womb
And the warmth of the grave
Are the warmth of my bones
As I whisper your name.

Geometrical Researches

If I had any natural aptitude for math,
I'd probably tell you something like,
"Since one and one make two and with
Two hands you count to ten lets
Count to twenty twice and chart
The curve with which your index finger
Smooths the wrinkles in my soul –
I'm sure its parabolic, for that's
The figure that I like the most, although I
Must admit I love your almond eyes
So maybe, an ellipse?" I
Start to wonder... would you
Wander towards me? If I was some
Asymptote, would you break the
Curve of your perfect figure at
Just one point, to touch my hand?
Or could I curvilineate myself enough
To describe the arc required for
A kiss?
I'd have to do the research, to be honest...

But I have never backed down from a quest,
And though I know that Euclid never got it,
Not Lobachevski, Apollonius, or Descartes,
And Ptolemy only taught me what it meant
To circle round a sun, Newton gave me
Reason to believe the infinite could be overcome
And so, I think, I may have cause to hope

That you and I might someday fall in love.

Reflections rather than reading Darwin

You drowned yourself –
That's the size & shape of the
Thing.
You polluted, poisoned,
All that bashful
Breathing out & in,
Breath like breath, to breath
Return –
I return:
A gentle breeze, flowing,
Floating,
Gurgling, gasping, reaching for
A hand never quite not there –
Choking, sprawling
On the only shriveled shift of dust
Remaining in this dusky town.
(Oh, but you...)
I have brackened –
(Oh, you)
I... betray?
(I am you)
I am you.

3:30 and Tomorrow

Somehow I came here,
To the corner of 3:30 and tomorrow,
(That poor excuse for a corner,
It's more hyperbolic than that);
I am facing jalapeno plants,
Questions about whether I should fall in love again,
And a last cigarette.
A gale bellowed behind me,
And somewhere in it you stood
Eating almond-butter.

I can see the universe in her eyes
Expanding out like Christmas,
And the spirit of Adventure
Was the scent she wore.

We flew cart-wheel-like down shaky streets
And tomorrow-lands
Where beer is not yet sold,
But cigarettes are cheap;
Where winds whip palm-fronds about our feet
Like Passion Sunday in reverse,
Like dawn was far away,
And we, the only creatures in this
Sleepy town,
Riding through the gates
On the flaming chariot of our victory.

I have not felt more alive
Than when the wind and stars whirled
Like drunken joy to hear your voice
And so wrapped your hair like harness
Round your face – you
Unharness-able thing –
As you flew head-first out the window
Because the door would take too long.

We stood beneath the Stars
And Yelled out to the Stars
Against the wind that blew our voices to the Stars
We called out to the Stars
We raised our lungs and so
Ourselves in chorus with that Blasting Breath
Of Holy Spirit rushing over
Mountain-tops and crests,
And when I showed you the cows-head in the sky
You showed me Betelgeuse
So I could learn exactly what it was
That burst so fully from your eyes –

You... supernova-bright.

You... gas-cloud-joy.

You... orb
Of endless.

You have made me love the night once more
Not because of darkness
But because light
Means much more when there is less.
Words mean more
When there are less.
Silence means more...
And I would have said more,
Would have wrapped around my hands
A rope and tied me to yourself,

If those winds had not ripped
A tiny hell-fire of a bat
And thrown it face-first against my lips
I think all of nature was jealous of me
And tried to give me rabies
So I couldn't kiss you,
Because it's heard every word you said since you were born

And I just started listening.

Besides, maybe all you really wanted
Was a beer.

Finality

Something before, here:
Ghosts trek out their repetitions
Before returning home,
And even rain, sometimes,
Stops reminding of a perfect kiss.
Time becomes a rythm –
A pattern, done
Over, and over, and over
Catching up us all,
Catching up us all like shoals
Catch up ship-wrecks,

Or like love catches up us all

Mid-Breath

Ash Wednesday

The dust begins to settle.
Ashes on our heads firmly describe
Descent, and practicing dissent
Becomes more difficult.

"Remember, man..."

Father,
I remember.

I remember large hands,
Folding in upon themselves
Like psalms prayed twice
Were not enough to hold you
In existence.

I remember sweating out a summer
Chasing baseballs
And the 'CRACK!'
When you sent them soaring
Into outerspace.

I remember learning that
Chess was a man's game,
But gambling was for children
When I bet you that I'd win.

I remember the smell of
Marlboro Reds – a brand
I still don't smoke –
And how much I missed it

When the cancer ate you away.

"Remember, man, that thou art dust..."

Father,
How could I forget?

Rain in a Dry Year

I. Interstate 5 North

The sky creaks out there –
Shaking down the sea-foam slopes
Scrawling out into the grass-fed land,
Writing large and tall the words "WIDE OPEN"
Onto all that lonely world.

"Congress Made Dust Bowl"

"No Water No Jobs"

Signposts spit gospel-truths at me
As flat-out 85 I fly through
Straight-shock blacktop freeways
An arrow aimed at home.
"Call your Mother."
This last sign shouts out from the roadside
And far off in the distance
I can see a sheep give birth.
Life comes so quick
That it hurts hard to keep.

I'm going home,
But everything I see is coming south.

II. San Francisco

Clarity is hard to come by here.

More often, fog rolls
Gently up the dizzy hillside streets,

Wraps round tall red towers,
And settles in the window-panes
And siding.
I was a child, once, leaning
With my nose against the glass,
Watching as the neighborhood
Settled underneath the sheets
And went to bed.

I was a child, once,
A child who lived everywhere but
Loved most the faded yellow carpet
Spilling down the stairs, loved it more
Than sunflowers in France,
Than clear lagoons in Trinidad,
Or the red clay wind of Mali.
I am coming home,
To let the slick-wet sidewalks know
That I am still alive;

I am coming home,
Seeking clarity.

III. Holy Cross Cemetery

I have not knocked upon this door
For 15 years,
Although I have stood before its oaken frame
And peeked into the window.

A decade and a half is a long time to
Miss somebody, you say,
Staring through me in a whiskey haze
And now I realize just how long it is –
Long enough for a community to
Build up around the flower-shop
That stood alone back then,
Long enough to be forgotten and forget

Those eyes that stand behind the counter
Making small-talk for $8.99 I spent
On flowers that I hope
Are nice.

But I still know this land,
This land that seeped into my bones and
Bled into my veins,
The gold-white shock of daisies
Sprouting out of graves
Dreamt from sleeping skulls beneath my feet;
So, standing by the slate-grey granite
Stone, I say that Rain
Is far more cruel than dust,
That dry years hold no storms, at least,
And floods rip life out of
Bleached bones and buried things;
And so this rain that rushes from my eyes onto your grave
Is cruel,
Because from you I tear my life away;
Now, I whisper words I never said
In all these years:

My Father
          is dead.

Now I must leave this place.

The Poet's Prayer

The Poet's Prayer

Lord, grant me eyes to see and ears to hear, that,
Seeing, hearing, I may speak
That Infinite Innocence raised upon the tree;
That Beatific, sleeping on my tongue.
Yes, Lord, show me truth and honesty in man;
Show me truly all the works of hands,
And honestly, the sadness, dwelling
Full and hard upon our human backs;
Show me beauty in this earthly tapestry
That spans across all ages;
Show me beauty, Lord, in tiny things.
And, oh God, when through all the years;
When, through all the nights and all those sunrise days
There comes, at once, the end of dusty streets;
Grant me then, Oh Jesus Christ, to reach my hand,
And touch thy untouched face.

A Flame

A flame of burnished bronze against the stair
Of sky, and space, and time, does beat
Upon that brilliant blue, that climbs in sheets
That creep to God to cry – and yes, to dare –
That trackless reach of timeless age, that age
That burst a changeless flame, a latticework
Of sunset, sunrise, red as death unshirked;
As red as lips depending on a name.
Oh, grasp this flame of mine, you Fullest All,
That whisper of a dawn upon my ear,
For I am naught but naught, and naught is here
That is of mine; make me to thee a thrall;
And then, when with this dying I have done,
Enfold me in thy flame, as though a son.

How to Write

For Patrick Conklin

First:
Don't. Plan. Anything.
Write a word, allow the next
To bubble up onto the page just like today
Slips into tomorrow
The way a woman slips out of
Her dress –
That is how you start.

Second:
Pretend tomorrow
Is a never, and that
Today really,
Really needs a singer
Before its gone,
Because you know it's only dead the last time
Someone says it –
So sometimes
Be a paramedic,
Beat yesterday's chest
Like its breath just might
Burp up again,
Drag fact
Into a fiction,
Immortalize mistakes,
Turn yourself into a page
That got scribbled
All over;

Third:
Learn to love that pain
You call a pen,
Learn
That every scratch,
Each crosshatch and mishap

Is a brutal beauty waiting for that moment
When you realize
That your Father's death
And ex-girlfriends,
Your failures in school
And problems with discipline
Are written on your skin
The way rain writes rivulets down mountains
And you better learn
to
Love them like a better half
Or you'll lose it, boy...

Fourth:
Never stop writing about
Wheelbarrows.

Fifth:
Wrap a mountain round your face
And breathe forever,
Scratch your chest with breaths like
Sandpaper,
Scrape them out of you
And super-glue them to the stars;
Bring the night sky home
To sleep on the refrigerator:
That is what you do.
You weave your life to
Shining light
Like flax to gold
Like all that is depends on what
Is told
In rhymes that don't quite make it
And words that sometimes forget
Exactly what they mean,
Like 'effulgent.'
And 'hypogriff.'
And 'eructation,' which
Doesn't mean what you would think;
That is when you'll know you've had a taste...

Sixth:
Become a cannibal
And eat your memory.

Make reality that little spot of nothing
Where it all began,
Say with force that all is one,
Forget your flesh, remember
All that was remains
But never happened;
Feast upon that everything,
Make your words turn back into
A blank unwritten page –

Erase.

Seventh:
Begin again, let
Yesterday become a yesterday,
Let tomorrow happen when it wants
And let today reach out its arms,
Grab hold of all that is
And ever was:
Write the word "love,"
Lovelovelovelovelove
Far too many times
And live it even more,
Get heart-broken,
Beat your self-respect into the floor
And realize that Love
Speaks everything;
So write love on
Everything you see
And anything you taste
And anything you speak and feel and remember and
Forget on your hopes and on your
Dreams and on your fears and on your joys
And on your mistakes and on your pain
And on your breath and on your

Breath and on your Breath
Write Love on Everything
Write Love
Write
Love
Write Love on Everything –

This

                          is how you write.

Lady of the Sea

I saw her by the seashore, singing there,
With salt upon her eyes, and in her hair
And on her lips the ocean hung like fire,
And on her song I hung, with some desire –
Some want I'd never lacked, she sang with grace,
Some Hope I'd never hoped, some life, some faith,
She sang the sea into my heart, I think,
For words are not so kind, nor eyes so deep,
Nor voice so strong, that with one word, so sweet,
She breathed away the cloud oe'rshadowed me,
And like some dream, I stepped down to her side,
And begged her, "Lady, teach me songs like thine:
Oh, let me close, to breathe your shining eyes,
Or give me leave to go, and leave to die."

California

My Home is the land of bleached bones picked bare,
Of rolling hills, of waves sprayed
In the shadow of sky-scraped cliffs
Climbing up, and up, and up to touch God's hand.
It is the smell of sweat and shit,
The smell of old and new, birth and death;
A bovine smell, the smell of dust and clay.

My home is sunburnt dry, a wrinkled face –
Each line, a staid defiance; each furrow, steadfast strength –
A regal quiet; A calm, triumphant gaze
Of land yet to be found, mountains burning in the blaze
Of cloudless skies, trod in no man's days.

My home is shouldered in the foothills,
Its breath, this wind upon my face,
That breathes the brown land deep into my lungs,
Breathes lemon trees, scrub oak, cactus flowers.
It is a wanderlust, a push for higher, and for higher
Until at last I, too, will soar and touch God's face;
Until I, too, become a circling bird of prey.

My home is hills and mountains, sunburnt neck and thirsty tongue;
Horses stamping wild, cows pondering their cud;
It is a land of life unbridled, of death unkept, unhinged;
A blanket, warm and peaceful, a mountain, proud and grim.

Somedays

Somedays, water pours,

Slips in through open doors,
Puddles, plops with little bubbles, bursting
Like wet kisses
When the rain finally came four years ago,
And you looked – beautiful.
Every moment that I've lived exists
In each juicy drop that suicides against
My windshield,
Boiling brake-lights onto wet glass,
Making me,
Silly Southern-Californian that I am,
Absolutely Terrified.

I don't know how to drive when I can't smoke,
So struggling to keep this cigarette alive
Reminds me of a woman that
Lasted for a year. I really tried,
And yea, it was really good for a little while
But then her smile started running
Like refrigerators,
Running like there was some place
To be that wasn't here, because here
There was only love; and when my arms
Wrapped round her body
Like a vines wrap round a wall
She felt –
uncomfortable.

So write this in your diary, your
Glossary – dammit, in the margins of your photographic memory
That Love is the mat that I lay at my doorstep.
So wipe your feet off and come on in
And I'll give you everything you need, and maybe

More than you can take,
And I've been told I'm gonna break if I
Keep shaking hands and bumming smokes
And yeah, I'm kind of scared that that's the case
Cause I've lost
A Lot –.

But every breath I take could be
My last
So I'm done living in the past,
And every morning when I wake I laugh
Cause just how cool is that?
I can bubble up my breath and make it joy,
I can make it dance around my room
Like spring rain, or perfume –
Like graduating high school,
Or realizing that a smile is just a smile,
And tears are just tears,
And a drop of rain on a green, green leaf
Is just a drop of rain on a leaf.
So, when I enter eternity, I know
I'm going to say, "God, I don't know
How I did,
I tried, sometimes, I guess,
But that drop of rain – Man,
You really did something pretty there."

So I'm here to tell you don't be afraid of love,
Don't be afraid of getting over stuff,
Because it never really goes – it sticks
Inside, like beehives, you honey-comb them till they're sweet.
You learn to cope, and then to grow,
But still your roots grow deep into that soil
And yeah, its pretty rough somedays,
But still you gotta smile…
Cause everyone I know has had it tough
That's not to say your pain isn't worth that much

No, it's everything...
But smiling at a stranger in the street
Could change
Everything...

Now, reach out for the things that you can never really touch,
Like a concrete sky, or distance
In between two hands.
Don't worry about getting there,
Worry about going, worry about
Getting out of bed and putting on your shoes;
Worry about love, and how each moment
Falls madly for the next –
My past is a bunch of time kissing itself.
They say that time moves in a straight line,
And maybe that's scientifically correct,
But what I really think is that my past
Washes round my shoes with every step I take
'Cause that's me – it's not gone, it's just reduced
It's just like roots, and they've taken hold
In me.
Like some cartography
Of every single person that I've ever been,
And everyone I've ever known...

But somedays,
Death
Is just death,
Like when you hold a little yellow chick inside your hands
And all at once you're ten;
And though you know it's all happened before,
Right now, it's not again – it's something new,
Like when the smell of rain makes me remember
Breaking curfew,
Like jumping in a puddle at the age of 23
Makes me remember being – three.
That's death, you say...

But is it really?

Because a smile
Is not a smile.
And a tear
Is not a tear.
And Death – is
Not
Just
Death:

It's Resurrection.
Every moment dies because it loves the next.

Morning

The sun is caught in every blade of grass,
Skips off the bushes, caught in o'er-hung trees;
And spackles light on every living thing
That grows, or moves, or thinks. I think
This spinning globe that turns us from our beds
And shakes off all the sleep, and warms our hands
With orange, red, and golden splattered plants,
More brilliant than Monet; this spread
Of clearest morn and sunlit fingertips
That slide so gentle o'er these golden hills;
This flower-scented, sweetest breeze that fills
The heart in me with love for all that is.
Oh, Glory be to God, who made the day;
Yes, Glory be to God for all He made.

Santa Paula Creek

Dry lands are where I rise –
Dust, cow-pies, scrub-oak scattered
Over foothills, juniper and sage-brush
Shatter senses, and I leave footprints
On them all – or they, on me –
Brown lands are where I came from,
Where I remain. There are fields
Thick with sunlight glowing gold
Into the grass, and this is where
I learned that love is something more
Than just a word, but by your side I
Learned that love is something more
Than hands, and life often comes
With mud.

When you walk between the orange-groves
And avocados, carrying a paint-ball gun
And telling stories of your prowess – or
Humiliations – you might miss it in the taste
Of laughter, but the breeze begins to comb your hair
About a hundred yards away,
And the smell of wet seeps into your
Bones; like some primeval spirit,
You awaken. Feet will move more quickly
Towards that sound of speech
That is not said, those words that last
Forever, but cannot be written:
Water pounding rocks into oblivion.

These are what I try to write –
An oak-leaf floating in a still pool,
Boulders carried to the sea in winter-time,
And falling off the fish ladder, so soon
Made impotent when the rain came.
A creek will change its course, but stay the same.

I have sat beside you

And bathed within you,
Danced above you
And laid within you;
I have learned my life from you;
And now I fear to leave.

Mariclare, my words are yours.

To the reader: I thank you with all of my heart.